LITTLE
BEE

© 2022 Quarto Publishing Group USA Inc.
Text © 2022 Anna Brett
Illustrations © 2022 Rebeca Pintos

First published in 2022 by QEB Publishing,
an imprint of The Quarto Group.
100 Cummings Center,
Suite 265D Beverly, MA 01915, USA.
T (978) 282-9590 F (978) 283-2742
www.quarto.com

Editorial Assistant: Alice Hobbs
Art Director: Susi Martin
Publisher: Holly Willsher

A CIP record for this book is available from the Library of Congress.

ISBN: 978-0-7112-7415-0

9 8 7 6 5 4 3 2

Manufactured in Guangdong, China TT062022

LITTLE BEE

ANNA BRETT

illustrated by
REBECA PINTOS

Hello, I'm Little Bee, a bumblebee
to be precise! I'm a few days old and
have only just emerged from my cell
in our home, the nest.

Let me introduce you to my
family and we can spend
the day together.

I have a big family—over one hundred sisters and a few little brothers live with me, plus our mom, the Queen!

The other babies and I start the day by cleaning all the wax cells in the nest. It's the first lesson we learn—to always keep our home neat and tidy.

8

My mom is the Queen of our tribe!

She is much bigger than us
so she's easy to find.

It is our job to take care of her
and the home so she has the
energy to lay more eggs and keep
growing our family.

We all have specific jobs to do to make sure
the nest is a safe, happy, and productive
place to live. Girl bees are called worker
bees, and as we grow up our roles change.

While we babies clean the cells,
my older sisters look after Mom,
and care for the eggs she lays.

They also fly out to collect pollen
and nectar for all of us to eat.

11

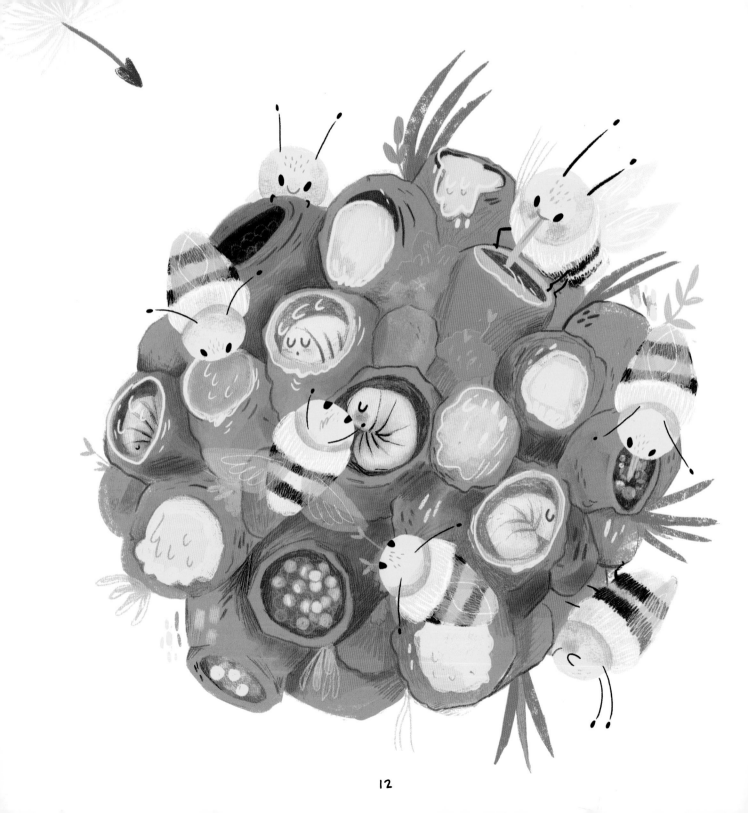

12

The nurse bees in our family take care of
the tiny eggs and developing babies in
the nest.

They get less sleep than the rest of us
since the babies need constant feeding.
But they love their job, and you won't
hear them complaining about being tired!

The oldest of my sisters have the best job—they get to fly out of the nest and buzz among the pretty flowers, collecting pollen and nectar for us to eat.

14

When they return, the way they smell
tells us all about the amazing sweet
scents of the best flowers!

The other members of our family are my brothers, the male drone bees.

They don't live with us for long, because when they are big enough they leave home to mate with young queen bees. They sleep curled up in flowers instead of in the nest.

Uh-oh, what's that sound?

We need to be alert, because occasionally a bird or a mouse might come looking for the nectar in our nest.

We females are each armed with a stinger covered in venom so that we can defend ourselves if needed.

Time for a break, and Mom
is telling us about how she
set up our home...

"When I was a young queen, I left the
nest in fall to mate with a drone.
As the temperature cooled, I found a
hole underground and snuggled down to
hibernate for the winter.

20

When the spring sunshine warmed me, I woke up and went looking for lots of sweet nectar to drink.

I then started searching for the perfect spot in which to build my new nest, and found this lovely shady corner of the woods."

Shh, let's listen to Mom telling the young queen bees about how to lay their eggs, ready for them to set up their own nests...

"The first step is to build your wax cells.

Fill a couple with nectar for you to drink, and the rest with pollen as food for the eggs.

Now lay your eggs on top of the pollen and they will hatch after three days."

23

Here are a couple of hardworking
nurse bees, taking care of the tiny eggs
the Queen has laid.

When the eggs hatch, they are called larvae.
They are fed "royal jelly," which is a special
liquid the nurse bees make.

As the larvae grow, they also eat the pollen and nectar in their cells. The nurse bees then cover the cells with wax.

In the enclosed cells, the larvae spin cocoons around themselves and change into pupae. And over a period of 12 days the pupae then grow and transform into bees.

Something exciting is happening today—our nest's young queens are emerging from their cells!

Eggs turn into young queens instead
of workers when Mom tells the nurse
bees to continuously feed royal jelly
to a few special eggs. This makes
them grow extra-large.

I'm hungry—time to raid the nectar pots! The oldest worker bees are in charge of making sure they've collected enough sweet nectar for all of us at home.

They store it in cells within
the nest, but it never lasts
long because we suck it up
with our long hairy tongues!

Mom always says "Don't forget
to collect the pollen!" whenever
someone leaves the nest.

Luckily, we are born with special pollen baskets on our legs!

When my sisters visit a flower for nectar, their furry bodies get covered in pollen. Then they can brush it all into the basket and carry it home, ready to unload.

It's been a busy day
for all of us and the sun is
setting now. Everyone returns
to the nest at night to sleep
and recharge. I'm going to
dream about the day when
I can fly among the flowers!
Goodnight, everyone!

FUN FACTS

Thanks for coming to visit me and my home!
I loved telling you all about our family.
Here are all the best facts about us bees.

BUZZ BUZZ BUZZ BUZ

- Bees have five eyes—two big ones and three little ones in the center of their forehead.

- Bumblebees beat their wings up to 240 times per second, and this is what makes their buzzing sound!

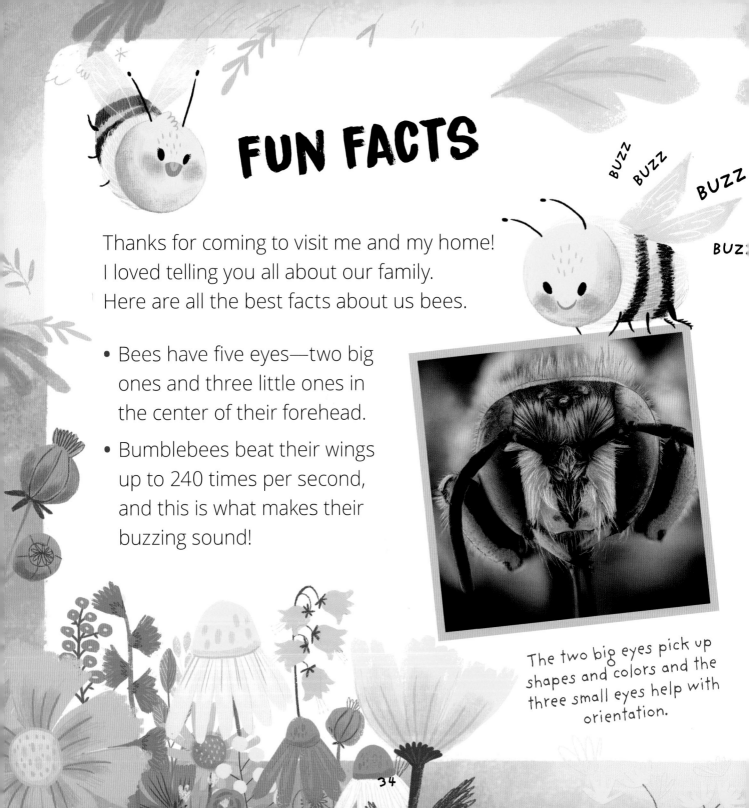

The two big eyes pick up shapes and colors and the three small eyes help with orientation.

- There are three types of bee: queens, workers, and drones.

- Their home is called a nest and it is made of little wax cells.

- Adult bumblebees mostly feed on nectar from flowers, while their larvae eat pollen.

Bees suck up nectar with their long tongue.

BEE PARTS

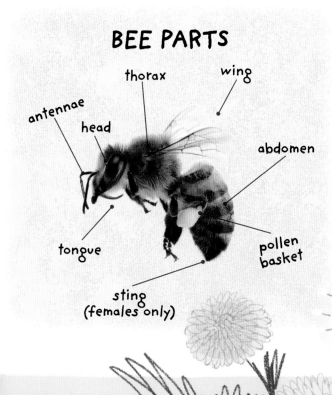

antennae
head
thorax
wing
abdomen
tongue
pollen basket
sting (females only)

- Bumblebees are insects with six legs.

- Bumblebees don't make honey—they don't store the nectar for long enough!

FLOWER FLIGHTS

Which route is this bee taking to fly toward the pretty wildflower? Follow the tangled lines to find out.

Can you spot the female worker amongst these male drones? She's the odd one out in the group!

POLLINATION

Bees play an important role in the pollination of flowers—this is when pollen from the stamen (male part) of one flower is transferred to the stigma (female part) of another flower to allow the production of seeds and new plants.

These bees are pollinating a pear tree

Bees move past the pollen on a flower to get to the nectar.

We bumblebees love flowers, but did you know that flowers love bumblebees as well!

Because bumblebees have furry bodies, pollen easily sticks to them when they brush past it on their quest to suck up the sweet nectar from flowers. Since they visit so many different flowers on their trips out of the nest, they move pollen from plant to plant without even realizing.

This bee is covered in pollen!

Other insects pollinate flowers too.

Plants attract insects to come and pollinate them with their brightly colored flowers and sweet-smelling nectar. Flowers come in all different shapes and sizes to attract different types of pollinators—butterflies, wasps, and beetles as well as bees!

BUSY BEES

It's always busy in a bumblebee nest! How many bees, nectar pots, and covered wax cells can you see in this picture?

This little bee is looking for a flower that has six petals, lots of pollen on show, and red and orange colors. Can you figure out which of these five flowers she should fly toward?

3

1

2

5

4

MAKE A BUMMBLEBEE

YOU WILL NEED

- Toilet paper tube
- Sheet of yellow paper
- Scissors
- Glue
- Sheet of black paper
- Black felt-tip pen
- Sheet of white paper

1 Cut a strip from the piece of yellow paper that is the same height as your toilet paper tube (about 4 inches) and long enough to fully wrap around it. Glue the back of this yellow paper strip and wrap it around the toilet paper tube.

2 Cut out two thin antennae shapes from your piece of black paper. They should be about 1.5 inches long and 1/8 inch wide.

3 Add glue to the bottom half an inch of these strips and stick them to the inside of the toilet paper tube to create two antennae.

4 Cut out two long black strips from your piece of black paper. They should be about half an inch wide and long enough to wrap around the body of your bee.

5 Glue the backs of these two strips of black paper and stick them around the lower half of your toilet paper tube. Leave a small gap between each strip so the yellow shows through.

6 Draw two big eyes on your bee using your pen, just under where the antennae are stuck. Now add a nice smile underneath.

7 Cut two wing shapes from your piece of white paper, add glue to one half of each, and stick to the back of your bee to create the wings.

OFF YOU BUZZ!

FRIENDLY FLOWERS

Did you know that there are over 250 species of bumblebee in the world, and the largest is almost over 1.5 inches long? However, sadly, many of the species are declining in numbers due to habitat loss. Luckily there are ways that humans can help bumblebees, and this is called conservation.

The largest bee in the world is Bombus dahlbomii.

Bumblebees play a key role in the reproduction of many of the plants that humans and animals eat because they are pollinators. Hundreds of years ago, there used to be many wildflower meadows so bumblebees had lots of pollen and nectar to feed on.

But now many of these meadows have disappeared as humans have built on them or the land has been changed into farmland. This means a lack of flowers and bees have a harder time finding the perfect spot to build their nest.

There's a simple way to help, though: just plant some bumblebee-friendly flowers! They love anything that flowers over spring and summer.

Here are some flower favorites... poppy, honeysuckle, coyote mint, rhododendron, prairie clover, wild roses!

QUIZ

Test your knowledge about bumblebees with this fun quiz. Can you score ten out of ten?

The answers are on the last page.

1. Bumblebees have two large eyes and how many small eyes?

2. Do males or females have a sting?

3. What is a bumblebee's home called?

4. True or false: only a queen bee lays eggs.

5. Which of these stages does an egg not go through before becoming an adult bumblebee: pupa, larva, tadpole?

6. What do bumblebees drink?

7. True or false: only male bumblebees collect pollen.

8. Bumblebees make what noise when they fly?

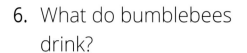

9. Who takes care of the queen bee?

10. True or false: bumblebees have eight legs.

ANSWERS

P 36-77

P 40-41

⑥ bees

① nectar pot

⑧ covered wax cells

Quiz answers

1. Three
2. Females
3. A nest (You may have heard the word hive as well, but that is where honeybees live!)
4. True
5. Tadpole
6. Nectar
7. False: only females collect pollen to bring back to the nest
8. Buzz!
9. Female worker bees
10. False: bumblebees are insects and have six legs

Picture credits

P34 Love Lego/Shutterstock. P35 bottom: irin-k/Shutterstock, top: Kerryn Price / Alamy Stock Photo. P38 bottom: enesayse/Shutterstock, top: MakroBetz/Shutterstock. P39 bottom: Jacqueline van Kerkhof/Shutterstock, top: Ihor Hvozdetskyi/Shutterstock. P45 nnattalli/Shutterstock. P46 Itsik Marom / Alamy Stock Photo. P47 bottom: Daniel Pahmeier/Shutterstock, top: Juniors Bildarchiv GmbH / Alamy Stock Photo.